# THE
## *Prayer*
# BOX

*"The Power of
Spiritual Discipline"*

## PAULA BRYANT-ELLIS

# THE PRAYER BOX

## "The Power of Spiritual Discipline" *Journal*

---

Paula Bryant-Ellis
MARY ESTHER RUTH, Inc.
6230 Wilshire Blvd. #895
Los Ángeles, CA 90048-5126
Email: maryestherruthblog@gmail.com
Website: maryestherruth.com

ISBN - 9781099672736
BISAC: Religion/Prayer

---

# A Note from the Author

Prayer is God's idea. Prayer is access to God. Prayer is not optional. God wants to talk to you! But you must show up, and you must be consistent. When you pray to the Father, don't worry about anything other than bringing your own personal aroma of prayer.

This is not a sprint to the finish, it's a kingdom marathon and only "By your endurance you will gain your lives." Luke 21:19

Remember, THERE'S POWER IN HABIT!

"Ask, and it shall be given you; seek, and ye shall find; knock, and it shall be opened unto you: For every one that asketh receiveth; and he that seeketh findeth; and to him that knocketh it shall be opened."

Matthew 7:7-8

# Prayers from the Heart!

*Remember why you started*

"*Pray without ceasing.*"

*1 Thessalonians 5:17*

*Grateful.*

"But my God shall supply all your need according to his riches in glory by Christ Jesus."

Philippians 4:19

*She replaced doubt with faith.*

*I love my private time*

*with the Holy Spirit!*

_Out do you today!_

"And the Word was made flesh, and dwelt among us, (and we beheld his glory, the glory as of the only begotten of the Father,) full of grace and truth."

John 1:14

What's behind your faith?

"If ye be willing and
obedient, ye shall eat the
good of the land"

Isaiah 1:19

*Faith is a power thrust forward.*

*"For we are his workmanship, created in Christ Jesus unto good works, which God hath before ordained that we should walk in them."*

*Ephesians 2:10*

Love is...

*"Let this mind be in you, which was also in Christ Jesus"*

*Philippians 2:5*

*Think BIGGER!*

"Verily I say unto you, Whatsoever ye shall bind on earth shall be bound in heaven: and whatsoever ye shall loose on earth shall be loosed in heaven."

Matthew 18:18

*I will not fail!*

"*Create in me a clean heart, O God; and renew a right spirit within me.*

*Psalm 51:10*

*Believe in You!*

"My flesh and my heart faileth: but God is the strength of my heart, and my portion for ever"

Psalm 73:26

She laughs and she prays.

"To appoint unto them that mourn in Zion, to give unto them beauty for ashes, the oil of joy for mourning, the garment of praise for the spirit of heaviness; that they might be called trees of righteousness, the planting of the Lord, that he might be glorified."

Isaiah 61:3

Rejoice!

"Every man according as he purposeth in his heart, so let him give; not grudgingly, or of necessity: for God loveth a cheerful giver."

II Corinthians 9:7

He qualified you.

"God is not a man, that he should lie; neither the son of man, that he should repent: hath he said, and shall he not do it? or hath he spoken, and shall he not make it good?"

Numbers 23:19

Be salt and light.

"But the Lord is faithful, who shall stablish you, and keep you from evil.

2 Thessalonians 3:3

_You cannot have what you refuse to build!_

# ABOUT THE AUTHOR

Paula Bryant-Ellis is a Los Angeles-based creator, writer, and director. Prior to returning to the entertainment industry, where she'd started her career as an accountant in television, she held multiple leadership roles in banking and finance, including Chief Operating Officer.

Paula is a wife (married 38 years), a mother, and an entrepreneur; therefore, she holds a deep understanding of the many challenges women face today in their faith and relationships, with their families, and in their careers.

**To find out more about MARY ESTHER RUTH,**

**please visit maryestherruth.com**

Made in the USA
Columbia, SC
26 August 2022

65647733R00089